UXBRIDGE COLLEGE LEARNING CENTRE

Park Road, Uxbridge, Middlesex UB8 1NQ
Telephone: 01895 853326/8

UXBRIDGE
COLLEGE

Please return this item to the Learning Centre on
or before the last date stamped below:

2 0 DEC 2001		
2 1 APR 2008		
⌐N 2013		
2 5 JUN 2013		

ARISTOTLE IN 90 MINS
PAUL STRATHERN

ARISTOTLE IN 90 MINUTES

Paul Strathern

ARISTOTLE
(384–322 BC)
in 90 minutes

Constable · London

First published in Great Britain 1996
by Constable and Company Limited
3 The Lanchesters, 162 Fulham Palace Road
London W6 9ER
Copyright © Paul Strathern 1996
The right of Paul Strathern to be identified as author
of this work has been asserted by him
in accordance with the Copyright,
Designs and Patents Act 1988
ISBN 0 09 475980 4
Set in Linotype Sabon by
Rowland Phototypesetting Ltd,
Bury St Edmunds, Suffolk
Printed in Great Britain by
St Edmundsbury Press Ltd,
Bury St Edmunds, Suffolk

A CIP catalogue record of this book
is available from the British Library

All translations are by the author.

Contents

Introduction

Aristotle was perhaps the first and the greatest of all polymaths. He is known to have written on everything from the shape of sea-shells to sterility, from speculations on the nature of the soul to meteorology, poetry and art, and even the interpretation of dreams. He is said to have transformed every field of knowledge which he touched (apart from mathematics, where Plato and Platonic thought remained supreme). Above all, Aristotle is credited with the founding of logic.

When Aristotle first divided human knowledge into separate categories, this enabled our understanding of the world to develop in a systematic fashion. But during recent centuries our knowledge expanded to the point where it was being seriously hindered by this categorization. Such systems of thought only allowed knowledge to develop along certain predetermined paths, many of which were in danger of petering out. A radically different approach was needed. The result is the modern world of science.

The fact that it took us over twenty centuries to discover these limitations in Aristotle's thought only goes to demonstrate his unparalleled originality. Yet even the demise of Aristotelean thought has given rise to many fascinating philosophical questions. How many more of these limitations have we yet to discover? How dangerous are these flaws in our way of thinking? And exactly what are they preventing us from learning?

Life and Work

On a promontory above the village of Stagira, in northern Greece, there's a rather uninspired modern statue of Aristotle. Its expressionless face gazes out over the lumpy wooded hills towards the distant blue Aegean. Aristotle's pristine white marble form, almost luminescent in the brilliant sunlight, wears a *décolleté* toga and sandals, and bears a slightly chipped scroll in its left hand. (This damage is said to be the work of a souvenir-hunting Argentinian philosophy professor.) Carved into the plinth in Greek are the words 'Aristotle the Stagirite'.

Aristotle was born at Stagira in 384 BC. But despite the statue, he didn't enter the world in the modern village of Stagira. According to the guide book this event took place in nearby Ancient Stagira, whose ruins are still visible. After my disappointing encounter with the statue, I set off to find them. The ruins were somewhere just down the road, I was told by a batman returning home from school. With a flourish of his black plastic cloak he indicated the road to the coast.

After an hour's sweltering walk down the long winding road to the coast, with the thunder rumbling ominously around the rocky hills above me, I was eventually given a lift to Stratoni, an eerie combination of deserted seaside resort and mining village. Ancient Stagira lay somewhere off the old road a bit further to the north, I was told by a carpenter who was repairing the closed café on the empty front.

Few cars travel on this road in October, as I was soon to discover. And the autumn storms in this region, when they eventually break, can be very severe. For an hour I sheltered beneath a narrow ledge of rock as a torrential downpour cascaded over the bare hillside – with no sign of ruins or vehicles visible in the flickering crashing gloom around me. Soaked to the skin, I raged to myself about the statue which had led me to the wrong Stagira. It was nothing more than a fraud. The modern village of Stagira had no claim whatsoever to be known as Aristotle's birthplace. Why, by the same token, they might just as well erect a statue of Joan of Arc in New Orleans . . .

Aristotle was born in 384 BC at Ancient Stagira in Greek Macedonia. In the fourth century BC Macedonia was regarded by the Ancient Greeks in much the same way as the modern French tend to regard Britain and America. But Stagira was not beyond the pale of civilization – this was a small Greek colony founded by the Aegean island of Andros.

Aristotle's father Nicomachus had been personal physician to Amyntas, the king of Macedon and grandfather of Alexander the Great. As a result of this connection, which had ripened into friendship, Aristotle's father seems to have become a rich man, acquiring estates around Stagira and elsewhere in Greece. The young Aristotle was brought up in an atmosphere of medical learning, but his father died when he was still young. Aristotle was then taken to Atarneus, a Greek city on the coast of Asia Minor, where he was brought up by his cousin Proxenus.

Like many an heir to a fortune, Aristotle soon began spending his inherited cash in determined fashion. According to one story he blew the lot on wine, women and song and ended up so broke that he was forced to join the army for a spell. After this he returned to Stagira where he took up medicine. Then, at the age of thirty, he gave it all up and set off for Athens to study at the Academy under Plato, where he remained for eight years. Later medieval hagiographers, determined to turn Aristotle into a saintly character, tended to ignore or vilify these unthinkable calumnies. And sure enough, there is another version of Aristotle's early manhood. According to this rather more boring (but admittedly rather more credible) story, Aristotle went straight to the Academy at the age of seventeen. Yet even some of the sources for this story allude to a brief 'hooray Henry' interlude of wine and Rosies.

Either way, Aristotle soon settled down to a period of intense study at the Academy, quickly establishing himself as the finest mind of his generation. Initially he was a student, but he was soon invited to become one of Plato's colleagues. It seems that, to begin with, Aristotle worshipped Plato. He certainly absorbed all the Platonic doctrine that was taught at the Academy, and his own philosophy was to be firmly grounded in its principles.

But Aristotle was far too bright to be a mere follower of anyone, even Plato. When Aristotle discerned what appeared to be a contradiction (or, heaven forbid, a flaw) in the works of his master, he felt it his intellectual duty to point this out. This habit soon began to irritate Plato, and though they appear not to have quarrelled the evidence suggests that the two greatest minds of their age soon found it politic to maintain a certain distance. Plato is known to have referred to Aristotle as 'the mind on legs', and to have called his house 'the reading shop'. This latter remark referred to Aristotle's famous collection of ancient scrolls. Aristotle was in the habit of buying up as many rare scrolls of ancient works as he could lay his hands on, and was one of the first private citizens to own a library.

The young academic evidently received a considerable income from his inherited estates, and soon became known in Athens for his cultured manners and gracious (if rather scholarly) life-style. Tradition has it that he was a weedy fellow, with spindly legs, who thpoke with a lithp. Perhaps to compensate for this he became a natty dresser, donning the latest fashion in sandals and togas, and adorning his fingers with tastefully jewelled rings. Even Plato, who was no pauper, envied Aristotle his library. Yet despite Aristotle's comfortable and refined way of life, his early works (now lost) were mainly dialogues discussing the base futility of existence, and the joys of the hereafter.

Aristotle had a natural inclination towards the practical and the scientific. This led him to view Plato's ideas from an increasingly realistic standpoint.

Plato believed that the particular world we perceive around us consists of mere appearances. The ultimate reality lies in a further world of ideas – which resemble 'forms' or 'ideals'. The particular objects of the world we perceive only derive their reality by partaking in this ultimate world of ideas. Thus a particular cat, such as the black one I can see lying on the chair, is only a cat because it partakes in the ultimate idea (or form) of cattiness; and it is only black insofar as it partakes in the idea (or ideal) of black. The only true reality lies beyond the world we perceive – in this ultimate realm of ideas.

Where Plato's approach to the world was essentially religious, Aristotle's tended towards the scientific. This made him disinclined to dismiss the world around us as unreal. However, he did continue to divide things into primary and secondary substances. Only for Aristotle the primary substances were the particular objects of the world, the secondary substances were the ideas or forms. Initially he did dither about which of these substances was in fact the ultimate reality, partly out of respect for Plato. (His old teacher had, after all, come up with this conception in the first place.) But gradually Aristotle became more and more convinced that he was living in the real world, and shifted away from Plato's view.

Over the years, Aristotle virtually turned Plato's philosophy on its head – yet, despite this, his metaphysical theories remain recognizably an adaptation of Plato's. Where Plato viewed forms as ideas which had a separate existence, Aristotle saw forms (or 'universals', as he called them) more as essences embodied in the substance of the world, with no separate existence of their own. Aristotle was to come up with a number of devastating arguments against Plato's Theory of Ideas – but appears not to have appreciated that these criticisms were equally devastating to his own Theory of Universals. Yet no one else seemed to notice this either. As a result, it was largely in the form of Aristotle's modified doctrine that Plato's theories were to become the dominant philosophy of the medieval world. Fortunately there were many obscure points and apparent contradictions in Aristotle's works, which gave medieval scholars food for endless controversy arising from different interpretations. It was these arguments over errors, heresies, schismatic misbeliefs and devil-inspired misinterpretations which kept alive the notion of philosophy, when to all intents and purposes the entire enterprise had died (or perhaps more accurately, entered a long Rip van Winkle period). Though it has been suggested that a number of these controversies arose from simple clerical errors – the result of medieval copyists inserting their own guesses in place of words which were no longer legible in the original worm-eaten texts.

In 347 BC Plato died, and the post of head of the Academy fell vacant. Half a dozen of Plato's most able colleagues were all of the opinion that there was only one man fit to take over this prestigious post. Unfortunately, each of them had a different man in mind (usually himself). Here Aristotle was no exception. To his disgust Speusippus, Plato's cousin, was eventually given the job. Speusippus is known to have been so bad-tempered that on one occasion he tossed his dog into a well for barking during his lectures. He is also said to have invented a harness to enable the porterage of kindling wood, and eventually administered euthanasia to himself after becoming an object of public ridicule during an exchange with Diogenes the Cynic in the Agora. Speusippus was hardly the intellectual equal of the man whose doctrines were to lay the foundations of all serious intellectual thought for the next two millennia – and on his appointment Aristotle left Athens in high dudgeon, accompanied by his pal Xenocrates (another disappointed candidate).

Aristotle sailed across the Aegean to Atarneus, where he had spent his youth. This was now ruled by the eunuch Hermias, a Greek mercenary who had managed to take over this corner of Asia Minor. On a visit to Athens, Hermias had been highly impressed by what he had seen of the Academy, and welcomed

Aristotle with open arms. Hermias was determined to make Atarneus a centre of Greek culture, and Aristotle now began advising him on the best way to go about this.

Aristotle's political philosophy consists largely of an examination of the different types of state, and how best they can be run. His understanding of politics is profound. This led him to adopt a pragmatic attitude, in direct contrast to Plato's idealistic approach. In *The Republic* Plato had described how a philosopher-king should rule his utopia (which, like any utopia, was in fact little more than a tyranny). Aristotle, on the other hand, described how to run an actual state – outlining effective courses of action that are often almost Machiavellian. Aristotle knew how politics worked, and knew that it had to be effective to be of any use at all. That is not to say he was devoid of ideals. On the whole, Aristotle believed that the purpose of the state was to produce and support a class of cultured gentlemen such as himself. Though he does understand that this is not always possible. For instance, in order to run a tyranny successfully its ruler must behave like a tyrant. In such a police state there would be no room for Aristotle's cultured elite. Yet at one point he does suggest that there is another way to run a tyranny. The tyrant can assume a religious pose and adopt a policy of moderation.

Some say that the latter is the approach Aristotle probably adopted whilst tutoring the tyrant Hermias. In my view, this is unlikely. Yet I'm not suggesting that Aristotle would have advocated the means for maintaining a full-blown tyranny – with all liberal cultural activity banned, the population kept in fear and poverty, set to work building great public monuments, with occasional interludes of war to keep them on their toes and demonstrate their need to maintain a great leader. (Aristotle's analysis remains relevant from Plato's philosopher-king to Saddam Hussein.)

Aristotle evolved his political philosophy during his later years, and at the time he was tutoring Hermias he probably adhered to the ideas expressed in Plato's *Republic*. If so, he may well have tactfully modified Plato's doctrine of the philosopher-king in this case. It was not necessary for a eunuch-tyrant to become a philosopher, instead he should just be sure to follow the advice of one.

Aristotle was now approaching middle age, and despite his dandyism (which can't have had that much scope, with only a toga and sandals to work on) he was considered very much the dry-as-dust professorial type. Then, to the surprise of all who knew him, Aristotle fell in love. The object of his affections was a young girl called Pythias, who is known to have been part of Hermias' household. Some say she was Hermias' sister, others that she was his adopted daughter – though some usually reliable sources claim that she was originally Hermias' concubine (which must have been something of a sinecure considering his sexual status). These contradictions suggest that she may well have been a palace courtesan. Was this an early case of the besotted professor falling for his Blue Angel?

Either way, Pythias wasn't a virgin when Aristotle married her, judging from his pronouncement: 'Once they have actually become married and call each other man and wife, it is quite wrong for a man or a woman to be unfaithful' – implying that prior to this it's okay. This pronouncement is found in Aristotle's remarks about adultery, and it appears that on such personal matters he was in the habit of generalizing from his own rather limited experience. In his remarks on marriage he asserts that the best age for getting married is thirty-seven for a man, and eighteen for a woman – precisely the ages at which he and Pythias were married. Brilliant though Aristotle may have been, imagination was not always his strong point.

This makes it all the more ironic that in his *Poetics* prosaic Aristotle sets out the most influential elucidation of literature ever written – while Plato, by far the most poetically gifted of all the philosophers, decreed that poets should be banned. (What was Plato trying to hide, one wonders.)

Aristotle had a high regard for poetry, claiming that it was of more value than history because it was more philosophical. History only deals with particular events, whereas poetry is closer to the universal. Here he appears to be contradicting himself, and echoing Plato's world view. However, Aristotle's celebrated assertion that tragedy 'arouses pity and fear so that such emotions are purged by the performance' remains a cardinal insight into the moving but problematic experience of tragic drama. Being a profound and essentially serious character,

Aristotle found himself out of his depth when it came to comedy. In his opinion, comedy is the imitation of inferior people, and ludicrousness is merely a painless form of ugliness. Aesthetics can only attempt to clear up the mess created by art, and theoreticians of comedy usually end up on a banana skin. Aristotle is no exception – observing that 'to begin with comedy was not taken seriously'.

Not long after his marriage Aristotle founded a school at Assos, and three years later moved on to Mytelene on the island of Lesbos, where he founded another school. By this stage Aristotle is known to have been deeply interested in the classification of plants and animals. One of his favourite haunts for specimen hunting was the shores of the all but landlocked Yera Gulf, whose still blue waters beneath Mount Olymbos are as idyllic today as they must have been then. In spring the slopes are covered by a multi-coloured carpet of flowers, and in Aristotle's day there would have been wolves, wild boar, lynxes and even bears in the mountains: the first naturalist's paradise for the first naturalist.

In his works on nature, Aristotle attempted to discover a hierarchy of classes and species, but was overwhelmed by the sheer volume of his researches. He was convinced that nature had a purpose, and that each particular feature of an animal was there for a function. 'Nature does nothing in vain,' he claimed. It was to be well over two millennia before biology made any effective advance on this, with Darwin's notion of evolution.

By now Aristotle had acquired the reputation of being the leading intellectual throughout Greece. Philip of Macedon had recently overrun Greece, for the first time uniting its bickering city states into one sovereign country, and he invited Aristotle to become tutor to his unruly young son Alexander. As Aristotle's father had been personal physician and friend to Philip's father, Aristotle was considered one of the family – and he felt obliged to accept this regal offer. Reluctantly he set out for the Macedonian capital of Pella.

Nowadays Pella is little more than a field of stones, with some pebble mosaics and half a dozen columns, beside the busy main road from Thessaloniki to the western Greek border. A surprisingly unimpressive spot, considering that this was the first capital of Ancient Greece; and later, after Alexander the Great launched his megalomaniacal campaign to conquer the world, it could even have claimed to be the first (and last) capital of the known world.

It was here in 343 BC that one of the finest minds the world has ever known set about trying to educate one of the greatest megalomaniacs the world has ever known. Aristotle was forty-two years old, and Alexander was thirteen – but not surprisingly it was Alexander who won hands down. The headstrong young pupil learned absolutely nothing from his tutor during the three years of their association. Or so the story goes. Aristotle was convinced of the superiority of the Greeks to all other races. In his eyes the finest leader would be a Homeric hero, such as Achilles, whose mind had been exposed to the latest advances in Greek civilization; and he believed that in man's mind lay an ability to subdue the entire world. There's no denying that Alexander bore an uncanny resemblance to this blueprint, even if he didn't turn out quite as Aristotle might have wished. But we can only speculate on this meeting of minds, about which curiously little is known.

What is known is that in payment for his services Aristotle asked Philip to rebuild his birthplace Stagira, which had accidentally been reduced to rubble during one of Philip's recent campaigns in the Halkidiki peninsula. And there's evidence that when Alexander was on his great expedition of conquest, he sent back assorted unknown plants and a zoo of exotic animals for his old tutor to classify. Horticultural lore has it that this was how the first rhododendrons reached Europe from central Asia. If so, Aristotle must have mis-classified this species: rhododendron means rose tree in Ancient Greek.

In 336 BC Philip of Macedon was assassin-ated, and the sixteen-year-old Alexander took over the throne. After speedily executing all other possible claimants, and embarking on a few preliminary *blitzkrieg* campaigns through Macedonia, Albania, up through Bulgaria and across the Danube, and down through Greece (reducing Thebes to a smoking ruin *en route*), Alexander then set off on his cam-paign to conquer the known world. In prac-tice this included north Africa, and Asia as far as Tashkent and northern India. Fortunately Aristotle's geography lessons hadn't men-tioned China, whose existence remained unknown to the west at this time.

Now that Alexander had other matters on his mind, Aristotle's presence was no longer required and he was allowed to return home to Stagira. But before he left Pella, Aristotle recommended his cousin Calisthenes to Alexander for the post of court intellectual. This act of generosity was to prove all but fatal for Aristotle. Calisthenes was a bit of a blabbermouth, and Aristotle warned him about talking too much at court before he left. When Alexander set out on his world-beating campaign, he took along Calisthenes as his official historian. But while they were fighting their way through Persia, Calisthenes appears to have talked himself into a charge of treason. Whereupon Alexander had him locked up in a portable cage. As Calisthenes trailed alongside the army in his cage, languishing in the desert heat, his body became covered with sores and crawling insects – until in the end Alexander became so sick of the sight of him that he threw him to a lion. But like all successful megalomaniacs Alexander had his paranoid streak: he blamed Aristotle for Calisthenes' treachery. Alexander is said to have been on the point of signing orders for Aristotle's death, but in the end forgot about this and set off to conquer India instead.

After spending five years in Stagira, Aristotle returned to Athens. Then in 339 BC Speusippus died and the post of head of the Academy once again fell vacant. This time the post was given to Aristotle's old friend Xenocrates, who was considered a suitably austere and dignified character, despite having once been awarded a gold crown 'for his prowess in drinking at the Feast of Pitchers'. (Xenocrates was to die in office twenty years later by tripping over in the night and falling into a water butt.)

Aristotle was so miffed at being passed over once again that he decided to found a rival school of his own. This he established in a large gymnasium beyond the city walls beneath Mount Lycabettos. The gymnasium was attached to the nearby Temple of Apollo Lyceus (Apollo in the form of a Wolf). On account of this, Aristotle's school became known as the Lyceum. The name lives on to this day, most appropriately in the French word *lycée* – though precisely why Aristotle's great school should also be commemorated in the names of ballrooms and theatres is not so clear. Aristotle's original Lyceum certainly taught a wide range of subjects, but ballroom dancing and acting were not to achieve fully fledged academic status until the twentieth century in the American Mid-West.

The Lyceum was much more like a modern university than the Academy. A new leader was elected to the student council every ten days; there were separate faculties which competed for students; and occasional attempts were even made to institute a time-table. The Lyceum undertook research in the different sciences, passing on its findings to the students – whereas the Academy was more interested in giving its students sufficient grounding in politics and law, so that they could become future rulers of the city. The Lyceum was the MIT (or even the Institute of Advanced Studies) of its day, whereas the Academy more resembled nineteenth-century Oxford or the Sorbonne.

The differences between the Lyceum and the Academy aptly illustrate those between the philosophies of Aristotle and Plato. Where Plato wrote *The Republic*, Aristotle preferred to collect copies of the constitutions of all the Greek city states and select the best points from each. The Lyceum was the school which city states turned to when they wished to have a new constitution written. No one tried to set up the Republic.

Unfortunately Aristotle's exhaustive study of politics had already been rendered practically redundant – by none other than his worst pupil Alexander. The face of the world was changing for ever: Alexander's new empire was bringing to an end the era of the city state, much as today the continental confederation of Europe may well be on the point of bringing about the effective end of the European independent nation state. Neither Aristotle, nor any of the galaxy of intellectuals gathered in the schools of Athens, appear to have noticed this great historical change – an omission on a par with nineteenth-century intellectuals from Marx to Nietzsche failing to foresee the supremacy of America.

Aristotle gave his lectures while walking with his pupils, and hence his school of followers became known as the Peripatetics (those who walk up and down). Though some claim that they received this name because their master gave his lectures in the sheltered arcade of the gymnasium (known as the Peripatos).

Aristotle is credited with the founding of logic (it was over 2,000 years before a logician of similar status was to appear), he was a metaphysician almost on a par with Plato, and surpassed his master in both ethics and epistemology. (Despite this, it's Plato who has the edge on him as an originator. Aristotle may have come up with the answers, but Plato was the one to see the basic questions which we should be asking in the first place.) Aristotle, whose most significant achievement was in the field of logic, came to see logic as the foundation on which all learning is based. Plato had understood that knowledge could be discovered by dialectic (conversational argument by means of question and answer). But it was Aristotle who formalized and advanced this method with his discovery of the syllogism. According to Aristotle, the syllogism showed that 'when certain things are stated, it can be shown that something other than what is stated necessarily follows'. For example, if we make the following two statements:

'All humans are mortal.'
'All Greeks are human.'

It can be inferred that:

'All Greeks are mortal.'

This is logically necessary and undeniable.

Aristotle called his logic 'analytika', which means 'unravelling'. Every science or field of knowledge had to start from a set of first principles, or axioms. From these its truths could be deduced by logic (or unravelled). These axioms defined the subject's field of activity, separating it from irrelevant or incompatible elements. Biology and poetry, for instance, started from mutually exclusive premisses. Thus mythical beasts were not a part of biology, and biology had no need to be written in the form of poetry. This logical approach released entire fields of knowledge, giving them the potential to discover whole new sets of truths. It was to be two millennia

before these definitions became a strangle-
hold, restricting the development of human
knowledge.

Aristotle's thinking *was* philosophy
through many centuries to come, and in the
Middle Ages it came to be regarded as gospel,
preventing further development. Aristotle's
thinking may have built the intellectual edifice
of the medieval world, but it was hardly his
fault that this eventually became a prison.

Aristotle himself would never have allowed
this. His works are littered with the kind of
inconsistencies which show a continually
questioning and developing mind. He preferred research into the actual workings of
the world, rather than mere speculation about
its nature. Even his mistakes often appear to
have poetic insight – 'anger is the boiling of
blood around the heart', 'the eye is made blue
by the sky'. In true Greek fashion he saw
education as the way forward for humanity,
believing that an educated man differed from

an uneducated one 'as much as the living from the dead'. Yet his understanding of the place of education was not that of a shallow optimist: 'It is an ornament in prosperity, and a refuge in adversity.' He may have ended up a bit of a pedant, but he gives indication of having known his share of suffering. He remained a teacher throughout his life, and never sought to hold public office – yet no man throughout human history has ever had such a lasting effect on the world, or is likely to do so until the ghoul who presses the nuclear button.

In this we are fortunate, for Aristotle seems to have been a good man. He saw the goal of humanity as the pursuit of happiness, which he defined as the actualization of the best we are capable of. But what *is* the best we care capable of? In Aristotle's view, reason is man's highest faculty. Therefore 'the best (and happiest) man spends as much of his time as possible in the purest activity of reason, which is theorizing'. This is very much an innocent professorial view of happiness: hedonism as a purely theoretical pursuit. Few in the real world would subscribe to such a view. It is arguable that Aristotle's pupil Alexander sought the actualization of the best he was capable of – inflicting suffering and death on countless thousands in the process. Yet it can also be argued that Aristotle sought to check such moral excesses with his famous doctrine of the Golden Mean.

According to this, every virtue is the mean between two extremes. Unfortunately this only leads either to mediocrity or verbal juggling. To call telling the truth halfway between telling a lie and correcting a falsehood is ingenious, but ethically vacuous. (Aristotle didn't maintain this, but would have needed to come up with something like it to fill the gap in his mean argument.)

During Aristotle's later years his wife Pythias died. Marriage obviously suited him, for he now married his maidservant Herpyllis, who was to be the mother of his first son Nicomachus. Then in 323 BC news reached Athens that Alexander had died in Babylon, at the end of a prolonged drinking bout with his generals. The Athenians had long resented being under the domination of the uncultured Macedonians, and at Alexander's death they gave vent to their feelings. Aristotle, who had been born in Macedonia and was renowned for having tutored its ablest son, became a victim of this wave of anti-Macedonian feeling. He was arraigned on a trumped-up charge of impiety, his accuser Eurymedon the hierophant citing the eulogy he had written twenty years previously on the death of his benefactor the eunuch Hermias of Atarneus. The mob required victims, and Aristotle would certainly have been sentenced to death. But Aristotle was not made of the same stuff as Socrates, he had no inclination towards martyrdom. Wisely he did a bunk from the city, to prevent Athens from 'sinning twice against philosophy'.

Yet this was no easy decision – it involved Aristotle abandoning his beloved Lyceum for ever. Deprived of his library and access to his research archives, the ageing philosopher now retired to some property in Chalkis which he had inherited from his father. This city lies thirty miles north of Athens on the long island of Euboea, at the point where it is separated from the mainland by a narrow channel. The waters of this channel are subject to an un-explained phenomenon. Despite the Aegean being virtually tideless, a rapid current runs through the channel, changing direction for no accountable reason as many as a dozen times a day. A persistent local myth has it that Aristotle spent many days racking his brains for an explanation of this phenomenon – and when, for the first time in his life he found himself defeated, he jumped into the water and drowned.

More reliable historical sources record that Aristotle died in 322 BC, at the age of sixty-three, a year after arriving in Chalkis. He is said to have died of a stomach illness, though one source claims that he committed suicide by drinking aconite, a poisonous extract made from wolf's-bane. This was sometimes used as a medicament in those days, which suggests to me an accidental overdose or self-administered euthanasia, rather than straight suicide. Though it's quite possible that his bitter disappointment at losing the Lyceum brought him to the point where he no longer considered life worth living.

Aristotle's will begins with the immortal words: 'All will be well, but in case anything should happen . . .' It goes on to outline instructions for the care of his children and the granting of freedom to his slaves. He then informs his executor that if Herpyllis wishes to get married again 'she should be given to someone not unworthy'. The author of this document comes through as an essentially prosaic, decent man, his character utterly unwarped by being the vehicle of supreme genius. He ends his will by requesting that part of the money he leaves be used to erect life-sized statues of Zeus and Athena in Stagira.

I detected no sign of these statues when I finally arrived at the scattered rain-swept stones of Ancient Stagira during the tail-end of a thunderstorm, on that unfortunate afternoon several years ago in Greece. As I blundered about on the god-forsaken hillside, I found myself reminded of Aristotle's insight into the nature of comedy. According to him, the ludicrous was merely a form of painless ugliness. Numb with cold, and not a pretty sight, I realized there was still some mileage left in Aristotle's thought, at least where the ludicrous was concerned.

Afterword

When Aristotle was forced to flee Athens in 323 BC, he left the Lyceum in the charge of Theophrastus. According to one source, Theophrastus had fallen in love with Aristotle's son who had been his pupil, but Aristotle evidently didn't consider this time-honoured occupational hazard disqualified his successor. Theophrastus ensured the continuity of the Lyceum after the departure of its founder, and its Peripatetic School of philosophers soon began living up to their name by wandering all over the Classical world, spreading Aristotelean philosophy wherever they went.

However, it was some three centuries after the death of Aristotle before his works were gathered in the form we know them today. Aristotle's *opus* can be divided into two groups – what he wrote for publication, and his lecture notes at the Lyceum (which were not intended for publication). Inevitably, the former has all been lost, and the only works of Aristotle which have come down to us are the latter. These were originally in fragmented form and covered hundreds of scrolls. They were organized into various distinct works by Andronicus of Rhodes, who was the last head of the Lyceum. It is to Andronicus that we owe the word 'metaphysics' – the title which he gave to a group of Aristotle's works. These originally had no title, and merely came after those on physics – thus Andronicus simply labelled them 'after physics', which in Ancient Greek is 'metaphysics'. The works in this section consisted of Aristotle's treatises on ontology and the ultimate nature of things. This subject quickly became identified with the label which had been attached to these works: metaphysics. So this word, which through the centuries has become synonymous with philosophy itself, originally had nothing to do with the philosophy it described. Just like philosophy itself, it began with a mistake and has continued to flourish as such ever since.

During the Classical era, Aristotle was not regarded as one of the great Greek philosophers (on a par with the likes of Socrates or Plato). In Roman times Aristotle was acknowledged as the great logician, but his other philosophy was largely eclipsed by (or absorbed into) the evolving Neo-Platonism. And over the centuries this was in turn mostly absorbed into Christianity.

Christian thinkers quickly realized the usefulness of Aristotle's logic, and it was now that Aristotle came into his own as the supreme authority for philosophical method.

Aristotelean logic was to remain the basis of sound theological debate throughout the Middle Ages. Up-and-coming monastic intellectuals indulged in nit-picking logical argument, the finest minds using this expertise to hunt out heresies. Aristotle's theologically unobjectionable logic thus became part of the Christian canon.

Yet parallel to this European Christian development of Aristotle's thought was another, equally important, eastern development – which was to have a profound effect on Medieval Europe.

During the early centuries of the first millennium AD the body of Aristotle's work remained lost to the Western world. Only in the Middle East did scholars continue to study the full range of his philosophy. The seventh century saw the rise of Islam, followed by widespread Arabic conquest throughout the Middle East. Islamic intellectuals quickly recognized the merits of Aristotle's works, discerning in them no conflict with their religious faith, and began interpreting them for their own purposes. Aristotle's teachings were soon absorbed to the point where almost all Islamic philosophy was derived from interpretations of his thought. It was the Arabs who first understood that Aristotle was one of the great philosophers. Whilst the Western world sank into the Dark Ages, the Islamic world continued to develop intellectually. Indicative of this rich heritage are the words which we have absorbed from Arabic, such as algebra, alcohol and alchemy, as well as our entire system of numbering.

Aristotelean philosophy was to be developed by two great Islamic scholars. Abu Aki Al-Husayn Ibn Abd Allah Ibn Sana (fortunately known to us as Avicenna) was born in Persia at the end of tenth century. Avicenna was to become one of the greatest philosopher-scientists of the Islamic world. His voluminous works on medicine were amongst the finest ever written, noble attempts to lift this subject from the quackery which it has never quite been able to forswear. Avicenna even attempted to remedy what he saw as elements of quackery in the works of Aristotle. He discerned various problems which Aristotle had overlooked, and even gave answers to these problems such as Aristotle might have given had he seen them in the first place. His attempts to render Aristotle's thought more systematic are masterly, and tie up many loose ends. Unfortunately much of this only closed off options which Aristotle had always wished to be left open. Aristotle knew he couldn't know everything – Avicenna felt otherwise.

The other great Islamic commentator on Aristotle was Averroës, who lived in twelfth-century Moorish Spain and became personal physician-cum-philosopher to the caliphs of Cordoba. Averroës was convinced that philosophy, in particular the philosophy of Aristotle, was the real way to the truth; the revelations of belief were merely a lower form of arriving at God. Reason was far superior to faith.

One day the caliph disturbed Averroës by

asking him how the heavens had come into existence. The philosopher was forced to confess that he had no answer to this question. (Not always a healthy intellectual position to adopt with a caliph who employs you to answer his questions.) Fortunately the caliph respected Averroës' honesty, and sent him away to find the answer in Aristotle.

For the next thirty years Averroës wrote an endless stream of commentaries and interpretations on Aristotle's work. (Though wisely he never came up with an answer to the caliph's original question: the caliph himself had already pronounced on this matter.) However Averroës did come up with several of his own answers to Aristotle, even providing arguments from Aristotle to support his point of view (which often contradicted Aristotle's).

This was just the kind of approach that appealed to medieval Christian scholars, who quickly perceived its uses in the persecution of heretics. Translations of Averroës' com-

mentaries on Aristotle soon began circulating
in Paris, the great centre of learning at the
time. But it was not long before the 'Averroists', as they became known, found themselves in trouble. Aristotle may have been
accepted by the Church, but these new teachings of his looked suspiciously unorthodox.
In the conflict between reason and faith, there
could be no doubting the supremacy of faith.
The Averroists found themselves faced with
the prospect of a heresy charge, and the only
way they could defend themselves was by
using arguments from the same source as their
heresy. Namely the writings of Averroës.

Fortunately the situation was remedied by
Thomas Aquinas, the greatest medieval
scholar of them all, who managed to patch
up a compromise. Reason must indeed be free
to operate according to its own inexorable
laws, but only from within the confines of
faith. Reason without faith was nothing.

Aquinas was deeply attracted to Aristotle,

and quickly recognized his supreme worth. He was to devote much of his life to reconciling Aristotle's philosophy with that of the Church. In the end, he succeeded in establishing Aristoteleanism as the philosophical basis for Christian theology. This was to be the making, and eventual breaking, of Aristoteleanism. The Catholic Church pronounced that the teachings of Aristotle – as interpreted by Aquinas – were The Truth, and could only be denied on pain of heresy. (A situation which remains in force to this day.) Much of Aristotle's philosophy concerned the natural world, and was thus scientific. Science, like philosophy, makes pronouncements which appear to be the truth – but later turn out to be wrong. They have to be modified, as our understanding of the world increases. By declaring the works of Aristotle to be the Holy Writ, the Church painted itself into a corner (and the corner of a flat earth, at that). The forthcoming conflict between the Church and scientific discovery was thus inevitable.

Aristotle is not responsible for this conflict between reason and faith, which was not satisfactorily resolved in Western thought until this century.

Despite the demise of Aristotelean thought, Aristotle himself has continued to play a part in modern philosophy. The contemporary philosopher of science Thomas Kuhn – a profound admirer of Aristotle – found himself puzzled that such a supreme genius could also be guilty of making a number of simple errors. For instance, despite some earlier philosophers realizing that the earth orbited the sun, Aristotle remained convinced that the earth was the centre of the universe – an error which severely restricted astronomical knowledge for over one and a half millennia. Scientific thought was likewise hindered by Aristotle's belief that the world was made up of four primary elements: earth, air, fire and water. Kuhn's study of Aristotle's errors led him to formulate his notion of paradigms, which revolutionized our thinking about the philosophy of science (and also had applications far beyond this field).

According to Kuhn, Aristotle was led into error because of the *way* he and his contemporaries viewed the world: the paradigm of their thought. The Ancient Greeks saw the world as consisting essentially of qualities – shape, purpose and so forth. Viewing the world in this way, the Ancient Greeks were *bound* to arrive at a number of wrong-headed conclusions, such as those which marred even Aristotle's thought.

The inevitable conclusion to be drawn from Kuhn's notion of paradigms is that there can be no such thing as a 'true' way of viewing the world (either scientifically or philosophically). The conclusions which we reach simply depend upon the paradigms we adopt: the way we decide to think about the world. In other words, there is no such thing as ultimate truth.

Key Quotations

We make war so that we can live in peace.
Nicomachean Ethics, Bk 10, 1177b, 5–6

Human good turns out to be the active exercise of the soul in conformity with excellence or virtue, and if there is more than one excellence or virtue, in conformity with the best and most complete. But this activity must take place throughout a complete lifetime, for one swallow does not make a summer, any more than one fine day. Likewise, one day or a brief flight of happiness, does not make a man completely blessed or happy.
Nichomachean Ethics, Bk 1, 1098a, 16–19

Tragedy is the representation of an action that is worthy of serious attention, involves greatness, and takes place over an extended time yet is complete within itself ... portraying incidents which arouse pity and fear, so that such emotions are purged by the performance.

Poetics, 1449b, 24–8

He who studies how things originated and came into being, whether this is the state or anything else, will achieve the clearest view of them.

Politics, 1252a, 24–5

Thus it is clear that the state is a creation of nature . . . And it is one of man's characteristics that he alone possesses a sense of good and evil, justice and injustice, and such, and the coming together of living beings who possess this sense makes a family and a state.

Politics, 1253a, 2–18

The notion of the state is naturally prior to that of the family or the individual, for the whole must necessarily be prior to the parts. If you remove the whole man, you can't say a foot or a hand remains, unless you look upon this as if it was made of stone – for it would only be dead. A thing is only understood to be what it is owing to its abilities and its power to perform them. And when it no longer has these abilities or power, it no longer remains the same thing, it merely has the same name. It is thus obvious that a city precedes an individual. For if an individual isn't sufficient in himself to form a perfect government, he is simply to a city what other parts are to a whole. And anyone who is unable to live in society, or doesn't need to because he is sufficient unto himself, must be either a beast or a god. Thus everyone has a natural impulse to associate with others in this way, and whoever founded the first civil society brought about the greatest good to humanity. In this way man is the finest of all living creatures, just as without laws and justice he would be the worst. For nothing is so difficult to eradicate as injustice perpetrated by force. But man is born with this force – which is both prudence and valour – and it can be used for both just and unjust purposes. Those who abuse this force will be the most iniquitous, lustful and gluttonous beings imaginable. On the other hand, justice is what binds men to the state; for the administration of justice, which consists of determining what is just, is the principle of order in political society.

Politics, 1253a, 25–40

Democrats maintain that democracy is what the majority decide, those who favour oligarchies believe that those with the most wealth should decide. But both these ways are unjust. If we follow what is proposed by the few, we soon have a tyranny. For if one person possesses more than any others, according to oligarchical justice this man alone has the right to supreme power. On the other hand, if superiority of numbers is the criteria which prevails,

injustice will be perpetrated by the confis-
cation of the property of the rich, who will be
in the minority and thus have no say. The
notion of equality, to which both parties will
subscribe, must therefore be taken from the
definition of right which is common to both.

Politics, 1318a, 19–28

The objects of mathematics are not substances in any higher sense than things. They
are only logically prior, not prior in being, to
sensible things. Mathematical entities can in
no way exist on their own. But since they
cannot exist in perceivable objects either, they
must therefore not exist at all or exist in some
special way which does not imply independent existence. For 'to exist' can mean many
different things.

Metaphysics, 1077b, 12–17

Where natural bodies are concerned, some
have life and some do not. That is to say,

some are able to nourish themselves, to grow and to decay. Thus every living natural body, which must be substance, must also be a complex substance. But since it is a body of a particular kind – that is to say, it has life – the body cannot be soul. For a body is a subject, not something predicated to a subject, and is thus matter. The soul is therefore substance in the sense that it is the form of a natural body, which potentially has life. Substance in this sense is actuality. In this way the soul is the actuality of the living body. But actuality has two senses, which are similar to the possession of knowledge and the use of knowledge. The actuality of which we are speaking is similar to the possession of knowledge. For both sleeping and waking require the presence of a soul – and waking is like the use of knowledge, whereas sleeping is similar to the possession of knowledge without using it.

De Anima, 412a, 17–26

It is obvious that there are causes, and many of them. These are discovered when we begin asking: 'Why did this happen?' This leads us back to several basic questions. When faced with unchangeable things, we are left asking: 'What is it?' For example, in mathematics it all comes down to the definition of a straight line or number or some such. Or in other cases we might be led to ask: 'What brought about this change?' As for instance in: 'Why did these people go to war?' The answer here could be: 'Because of border raids.' Or it could be because what the thing itself is for: in other words they fought for dominion. In another category, where things come to be, their cause will be matter.

Evidently, these are the causes. There are several different types of cause, and anyone who wishes to understand nature should know how to uncover them. In fact, there are four different types: matter, form, whatever brings about the change, and whatever the thing is for.

Physics, 198a, 14–24

Thus motion, being eternal, if there is a prime mover it too must be eternal . . . and here it is sufficient to assume there is only one mover, the first to set in motion stationary things, and this being eternal will be the principle of motion for all other things.

Physics, 259a, 7–14

Aristotle wrote and thought so originally about so many things that he was bound to get a few of them wrong:

People whose nostrils have thick extremities are lazy, just like cattle. Those who have thick ends to their noses are insensitive, just like boars. On the other hand, people who have sharp-ended noses are easily angered, much like dogs. However, those with round flat ends to their noses are magnanimous, in the same way as lions. People with thin tips to their noses are like birds; but when their nose is hooked and juts out straight from their forehead they are liable to shameless behaviour (just like ravens).

Physiognomics, VI, 28–36

Aristotle did much to establish scientific investigation and categorization. His achievements are astonishing, especially when one considers much of the current evidence and material in this field – some of which he recorded:

In Arabia there is said to be a species of hyena which paralyses its prey by its mere presence. If this hyena steps into the shadow of a man, it not only paralyses him but renders him completely dumb . . . There are two rivers in Euboea. The cattle that drink from the one called Cerbes turn white, and those that drink from the one called Neleus turn black . . . The river Rhenus flows in the opposite direction to other rivers, running to the north where the Germans live. In the summer its waters are navigable, but in the winter it is frozen with ice, so that the people can walk on it like land.

On Marvellous Things Heard, 145, 168

Chronology of significant philosophical dates

6th century BC   The start of Western philosophy with Thales of Miletus.

end of 6th century BC   Death of Pythagoras.

399 BC   Socrates sentenced to death in Athens.

c.387 BC   Plato founds the Academy in Athens, the first university.

335 BC   Aristotle founds the Lyceum in Athens, rival school to the Academy.

324 AD   Emperor Constantine moves capital of Roman Empire to Byzantium.

400 AD   St Augustine writes his

Confessions.
Philosophy absorbed into
Christian theology.

410 AD   Sack of Rome by Visigoths
          heralds start of Dark Ages.

529 AD   Closure of Academy in Athens
          by Emperor Justinian marks
          end of Hellenic thought.

mid 13th Thomas Aquinas writes his
century   commentaries on Aristotle. Era
          of Scholasticism.

1453   Fall of Byzantium to Turks, end
          of Byzantine Empire.

1492   Columbus reaches America.
          Renaissance in Florence and
          revival of interest in Greek
          learning.

1543   Copernicus publishes *De
          revolutionibus orbium
          caelestium* (On the Revolution
          of the Celestial Orbs) proving

mathematically that the earth revolves around the sun.

1633   Galileo forced by Church to recant heliocentric theory of the Universe.

1641   Descartes publishes his *Meditations*, the start of modern philosophy.

1677   Death of Spinoza allows publication of his *Ethics*.

1687   Newton publishes *Principia*, introducing concept of gravity.

1689   Locke publishes *Essay Concerning Human Understanding*. Start of Empiricism.

1710   Berkeley publishes *Principles of Human Knowledge*, advancing Empiricism to new extremes.

1716   Death of Leibnitz.

1739–40   Hume publishes *Treatise of Human Nature*, taking Empiricism to its logical limits.

1781   Kant, woken from his 'dogmatic slumbers' by Hume, publishes *Critique of Pure Reason*. Great era of German metaphysics begins.

1807   Hegel publishes *The Phenomenology of Mind*: high point of German metaphysics.

1818   Schopenhauer publishes *The World as Will and Representation*, introducing Indian philosophy into German metaphysics.

1889   Nietzsche, having declared 'God is dead', succumbs to madness in Turin.

1921   Wittgenstein publishes *Tractatus Logico-*

Philosophicus, claiming the 'final solution' to the problems of philosophy.

1920s   Vienna Circle propound Logical Positivism.

1927   Heidegger publishes *Sein und Zeit* (Being and Time), heralding split between analytical and continental philosophy.

1943   Sartre publishes *l'Être et le néant* (Being and Nothingness), advancing Heidegger's thought and instigating Existentialism.

1953   Posthumous publication of Wittgenstein's *Philosophical Investigations*. High era of Linguistic Analysis.